Calling Home

Christee Gabour Atwood

Always,

C. Atwood

D1715597

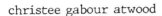

First Printing: 2022
ISBN: 9798773093213

Christee.net
Christee.Atwood@gmail.com
Louisiana, USA

For our mothers

Table of Contents

Chapter One

Where to Start?

Cemeteries live on the outskirts of town. I guess the land is cheaper. Also, we don't want the reminder of our impermanence staring us in the face every day.

Come to think of it, I guess that's why a cemetery works so well on church grounds. There, the reminder is appropriate. Probably good for attendance too.

On this autumn morning, the mist hung over the grounds so densely that the flowers looked more like tiny Christmas lights flickering through the haze as they caught the rising sun.

I made my way to the stone. I knew the way by heart now. In fact, I could almost see my regular path thinned in the wet grass.

And then I was in my spot and time fell away. Sitting at the foot of Mom and Dad's bed. Afraid of the lightning and begging to come stay with them till the storm had passed.

If I believed in such things, I could imagine our cemetery neighbors chuckling at the childish fears. They knew there were worse things than lightning. And they knew there were things that made the lightning worth every shiver.

I sat in the cemetery, on the wet ground, at the foot of my parents' spot. Yeah, I knew I was spending way too much time here, but it seemed the only place I felt at home now.

Our family home had been torn down and replaced with an extra driveway to a neighbor's house. Our other regular places were either closed or haunted by replays of moments, both happy and unbearably sad. And sometimes they were both.

And I? Well, I just wasn't sure who I was anymore.

The two people who loved me unconditionally were gone. And I had never been a member of that club. I had all kinds of problems with me.

Mainly, it seemed that my purpose had been to be their child. Period. Yes, I was a writer. Yes, I had jobs. Yes, I experienced things.

But I did it all through the eyes of their child. And now they were gone and honestly, I didn't know how to see things anymore. I was blind.

So, this blind used-to-be writer sat in the cemetery and cried, imagining herself in a scene from a movie so maudlin that she was embarrassed just picturing the camera angles and shots. But the sorrow had become a familiar comforter and she was loathe to give it up.

I sat for somewhere between ten minutes to three days and finally made myself stand. And yes, there was the creaking of bones. I'm over 60 now and it's hard to do anything without creaking. Or some sort of noise. Nobody told me aging included its own soundtrack.

I loaded my rear into a car that I had decided was too low for the size of that rear but didn't have the energy to change. The rear or the car.

As I drove back into town, I scanned the landscape. Still had non-stop trees here. The trees that were supposed to be here. Not the ones a person decided belonged. And weeds. There were lots of tall, primitive-looking weeds.

Have you ever noticed how beautiful weeds can be? They have flowers of their own, but we don't give them enough credit.

Weed flowers. I can see how that could be a negative if you sent them in a birthday bouquet.

But I digress. Much of my life has been a digression, so why should this story be any different? But most of my life has also been a fabrication, and this story is too real.

Chapter Two

The Gladiola

As I was driving with the windows open and a nice breeze whipping gray strands into my eyes, I noticed an old motel that had been mostly reclaimed by nature. I remembered the Gladiola. I slowed down. I couldn't pass.

I pulled into the remains of a gravel parking lot.

The Gladiola Motel had always had a bit of a reputation. Like it was made for cheap afternoon encounters. Now it was covered by vines, small trees, and a smattering of unidentifiable animal nests.

I'd never actually been inside of it. But the part of it I remembered was to the right of the building. And I couldn't believe it was still there.

Because, to the right of the Gladiola Motel was a phone booth. Yes, a real actual red and clear glass phone booth. Still standing.

The same phone booth we piled people into in the 70s when we were determined to break a world's record. Mom had laughed so hard at that. She maintained records were temporary, and she was looking for permanence in the world.

But nonetheless, the phone booth itself mocked us by its apparent permanence. I sneaked up on it, expecting it to disappear into the trees. But it stayed.

Holy crap. There was actually a phone still on the wall of the booth. Still kind of shiny. I pulled out my phone to take a picture of it. The irony was not lost on me.

I touched it, thinking it would vanish.

It didn't.

I felt the coolness of the handset and then did what anyone would have done in the 70s. I reached into the tray to check for spare coins. I discovered a nickel.

A nickel from the past. Magical. Just magical.

And on a whim, I did the unthinkable. I picked up the handset from that dinosaur and held it to my ear as I dropped the nickel in the slot.

Whoa. A dial tone? That was not possible. But there it was. A dial tone. I laughed. A dial tone from the 70s?

So, what do you do when you experience a moment that you never thought would happen again? You go along with the experience, right?

I thought out loud. "Okay, I could call 911. Nope. That might actually go through and then how do I explain that to the judge? I could call the time and temperature number, but I don't remember what it was."

I stopped and thought while staring at the dial and considered the numbers I used most regularly. The ones that didn't exist anymore. Like the number to my old family home.

"What the heck." The numbers came back to me as clearly as if I were still a youngster calling for a ride home from an ecology club meeting.

I fumbled, realizing I'd lost the skill of dialing. I heard the familiar sound of the tumbling and connecting of wires. I heard the click.

Holy crap. I heard the click. The sound of the phone receiver being picked up. Who had our old number? And the voice came from far away.

"Hello."

I couldn't respond.

"Hello?"

The voice. I couldn't breathe.

"Is anyone there?"

I didn't know if I was there or not. I was shaking so hard the phone was knocking me in the side of the head. I tried to make a sound, but no luck. Not even a cough came out. I stared at the receiver, at the dial, at the lost woman reflected back at me in the silver chrome of the phone body.

I hung up.

It was my mother. And I hung up on her.

Chapter Three

Missed Opportunities

I cried all the way home.

If my husband noticed my red eyes, he graciously ignored them. He did that a lot these days. He knew where I'd been. Even when I gave feeble excuses like going to the store and then came home without a bag. He allowed me my subterfuge.

"Out early. Good for you. Would you like some coffee?"

I nodded.

"Plans for today?"

I shook my head.

"Okay. Well, if you need me, I'm a phone call away. Or closer if you want."

Thank goodness for a man who knew when I needed space and silence. I smiled weakly and nodded as he headed out the door of our old historic home. The home we had bought a dozen years ago to restore. Then I had lost the will to restore anything. Including myself.

I curled up in a ball in bed and opened my phone to look at the picture of the opportunity I had missed. Damn. I guess I hadn't actually taken it. I really needed to learn how to work my phone's camera.

So that made me cry all the harder and the rest of the day was a haze. I remember some soup. I remember a cat trying to get my attention. I remember recognizing that I needed to take a shower. But those were just thoughts. No action. Just tissues and my grief comforter. And the thought that not waking up wouldn't be such an awful thing.

Chapter Four

The Connection

The next morning was much the same. Hazy skies. Mist. And me trying to decide if I dared to drive to the cemetery. Or more to the point, to the Gladiola. I dared.

My visit to the cemetery was shorter than usual. I was anxious. I drove into the gravel in front of the deserted Gladiola and imagined that it already looked older than it had yesterday. Such a loss. It was reminiscent of a different era. I could almost hear the big band tunes seeping out from the little café next to the lobby door. Yep, that was definitely 'Sentimental Journey.'

But my interest wasn't there. I wanted my phone booth. I went back.

I had a nickel in my hand, but I needn't have bothered. There was a nickel in the change tray again. I didn't question it. I just picked up the receiver and held the coin and thought.

I had considered this since yesterday. What would I do if this worked again? What would I say? What would the other end say?

The dial tone was insistent, so I traced the numbers to childhood again. After five rings the phone was answered by a breathless woman. Oh yes, I remembered. No answering machines in those days.

The breathless woman spoke, "Hello."

I managed a grunt.

"Can I help you?"

It was the voice of my mother. Not the way I remembered from the last dozen years of her life. Not faint and uncertain. Not raspy and breathy. It was strong and vibrant. And a bit impatient.

"Who is this? I am going to hang up..." I remembered that tone.

I cut her off. "I'm sorry." My wheels were spinning, but they were slow. "I wasn't sure I had the right number."

"Whom are you calling?" Of course, she would use proper English.

"Uh. Well, I'm calling to talk to a friend of Norene Simpson. She's my cousin." I silently hoped Norene had a cousin.

"Norene! How wonderful! How is she?"

This was so surreal. And that question was a hard one to answer. Norene had passed over 50 years prior. I assumed she was okay with that, so I answered, "Fine, thank you. I'm…"

Holy crapoley. Who am I? Do I tell her this is her daughter? Do I really feel like having her next call be reporting a crazed person to the sanitarium?

"I'm Chris."

"Well, hello Chris, cousin of Norene. And why are you calling?"

"I'm a writer. And she told me you were a really good writer and maybe you could give me some help."

I have no idea where that came from, but it was the biggest thing that Mom and I shared. We had been sisters as writers. Both fighting battles against the blank page since I was old enough to pound out chapters on her cast iron Royal typewriter.

"A writer? Well, that's exciting. I don't know why she told you I was good. I just knock out little stories to help pay bills. I write mostly for religious magazines and newspapers."

"She said you were amazing." Without even realizing it, I found that the discussion had switched and I was telling my own truth to her. Possibly for the first time. "She said you had a gift like no one she had ever seen. You brought truth to the page. She called you authentic."

She was silent and I could feel her soaking in the compliment. "I've always wanted to hear that about my writing. I'm so happy someone felt that in my words."

"She did. She told me she thought you were great and wished you would write more."

"I wish I wrote more too. But having six children keeps that from being too much of a possibility. They keep me pretty busy."

"You have six children?"

"Yes. In fact, the youngest shares a name with you. Although we call her Christee."

"Oh." I had no words.

"Yes, she's a special one. But right now she seems to have a diaper full, so I think I might have to close out our phone call. She's quite crabby when it comes to discomfort."

I laughed out loud. It was a sound that was unfamiliar to my ears. I hadn't heard it in so many years. Not real laughter. Not the kind that reaches beyond your throat.

"I can imagine she is." But I didn't want to hang up. I didn't want to lose this. I paused.

"But that doesn't mean we can't visit again. Anytime you'd like to call, I'll be glad to answer any questions I can help with. I love encouraging new writers. And I get the feeling you're a very special sort of writer."

I glowed. I breathed heavily. Okay, maybe I hyperventilated a little. But I choked out, "I'd really like that."

"Wonderful. I'll look forward to your next call. And even though she is wailing in the background now, I'm sure Christee will too. Have a nice day."

The phone clicked dead. No dial tone. No wailing baby. But it didn't matter. I'd just been invited to writing lessons with my mother. And this time I wasn't going to miss out.

Chapter Five

Discussing The Battle

There was no decision process anymore. The next morning, I hopped out of bed and into the shower. I can't tell you how long it had been since I could apply the word 'hop' to anything I'd done. Then I actually brushed my hair and dressed like I was going someplace special.

My husband didn't question. He knew there was an important transformation happening. I think he was just glad to see me out of the bed. And the house.

The car led me on my regular route to the cemetery. A brief visit with my parents' memorial. And then, as if it had been driving it for years, the car took me straight to the Gladiola.

Boy, it was a rough looking little building, but it looked like heaven to me. I ran to the phone, found my nickel, and dropped it in. Thank god, it worked again. I feared it might not, but I hadn't allowed myself to fully consider that possibility.

I dialed. I listened. I cheered in my mind as the click of the receiver being picked up told me I had connected.

"Hello."

It was definitely the right number. "Hi M... Mrs. Gabour. It's Chris."

"Chris. I'm so glad to hear from you again. And don't call me Mrs. Gabour. We're old friends now. Just call me Ruth."

"Ruth." That sounded strange coming off my tongue. Never in my life had I called her that name.

"That wasn't hard, was it?" Why did it seem like she was asking something more? But that was just my imagination in overdrive, of course. After all I was on a phone call to the past. Imagination was probably a key ingredient here.

"No. It's just I'm younger and I was taught…"

"You don't sound that much younger. May I ask?"

"Sixty-two."

"Well, actually you're a number of years ahead of me. So, I think Ruth will do quite nicely."

"Okay, Ruth."

"So, what's our writing question for today?"

I had totally forgotten that we were talking about writing. I had done so little on the page lately that it wasn't in the front of my thoughts like it used to be. In fact, I guess you could call it a drought. So that seemed like a good starting point.

"I'm blocked. I can't write anymore." As I began, words started tumbling on top of each other. I know I sounded a bit crazed, but I blurted onward. "I went through some tough things lately and it seems like all my creativity dried up inside me. I just don't feel like it's even worth the battle with the blank page anymore."

"The battle with the page." She laughed softly. "I use that term frequently. But you can't let it give you excuses."

"Excuses."

"My dear, the blank page is the only battle worth fighting. There's really no such thing as writer's block, you know. That just means you're trying to write the wrong thing. There's a real story to be told and you're not writing it. So your mind shuts down and refuses to write anything."

"The wrong thing?" That was what I keyed in on.

"The wrong thing is the thing you feel you should write about. The thing you think is useful or commercial or a good possibility to sell. But it's not your story. Your story is the one that nobody in their right mind would write. Because you know writers aren't in their right minds."

I laughed. "Oh, yes. How well I know."

"Your story is the one only you can tell. It's built from your experiences, your perspective, your memories, and mainly your mistakes. And it's the one that hurts to write."

"I thought writing was supposed to be fun."

"There was a quote someone said that I agreed with. It said something about writing not being fun. Having already written is the fun part."

"I remember that quote."

"I thought you might. We're very much alike, aren't we?"

"I always thought so."

"What?" She questioned.

"I mean, I think so." I paused, "You really don't believe in writer's block?"

"Do you, really? I mean, if the doctor said he was blocked and didn't feel like doing your operation, would you let him off the hook? Writer's block is an escape route. And if we take it, we're not writers anymore. We're just fugitives from our purpose."

I wanted to cry. This was the kind of talk I'd wanted to have with Mom for so long. But my desire to cry seemed to kick off a tiny wail in the back of my mind. Then I realized it wasn't in my mind.

"There goes Christee. She's got a strong voice, doesn't she?"

"I like it."

"Good. I think it's a voice that will take her far. I bet she's got some things to say."

"I'm sure. Once you can get her past that diaper stage."

"Yes. Which apparently needs to be changed right now. Shall we talk more later?"

"Can we, please?"

"Of course. I'm enjoying this."

"Me too."

"Have a very special day, Chris."

"I will. Thank you, Ruth."

The silence on the other end of the line didn't feel hopeless like it did before. Now it felt like opportunity.

And when I got home, I picked up my journal and began hurriedly scribbling phrases from our discussion. I felt like these were going to be some of the most important notes of my life and I wasn't going to lose a word of them.

Chapter Six

Gladiolas and Guilt

Strangely, that feeling of elation carried through the rest of my day and night. I captured thoughts and phrases that delighted me in my journal. I sketched a very bad picture of my cat. I colored it in with crayons.

It was as though all my creative voices were waking up at one time. None of them were great, but they were all part of me and it felt freeing to see them come out to play.

The next day I was up even earlier. Showered and dressed and out the door before the sun even had a chance to show up. It was a little tricky locating the drive into the Gladiola in the dark.

And then I realized that I had gone to the old hotel instead of the cemetery.

For a long moment I sat in my car, the guilt washing over me. I couldn't believe I had ignored my parents' resting place to come here instead. It darkened the pleasure of my anticipated call.

While I thought less of myself for letting go of that visit to their monument, I still refused to let go of my call. Could this be how addiction feels? Fear mingled with excitement, but also shame that we could be this selfish?

The thoughts muddled my mind as I picked up the phone. But a sweep of my finger told me the nickel was waiting and I scooped it up and dropped it in. The clink sounded a bit deeper than before, but I dialed and listened. The call still went through.

She picked up on the first ring.

"Hello."

"That was fast."

She chuckled gently. "I felt that you would be calling. I thought you might need some perspective today."

"How'd you know that?"

"People have vibrations. When you listen closely, you not only hear them, you feel them. Today your vibrations are deeper. Slower. Like you're troubled."

"I didn't realize you thought about things like vibrations."

"Of course. How can you ignore the very things that set off the waves we create in the universe?"

"But that sounds so new age."

"New age?" I couldn't tell if that was confusion or laughter in her voice.

"Never mind. It's just a term I heard."

"Well, here's something to consider. There's nothing new in the world. We can give it a new name. We can label it new and improved. But it's still just building on the old. The foundation that we've already created."

"What if that foundation was wrong?" I felt this conversation taking an unexpected turn.

"The foundation is never wrong. Do we ever wake up and say, "I want to create something totally false that will set the world in the wrong direction? I don't think so.

Instead, we try to create foundations that will last and prove our lives worthwhile. That's our purpose.

Although sometimes our methods get a little off kilter. That's to be expected. We're all crazy, remember?"

"But some people want to erase those off kilter moments." I'm not sure where that thought came from. Maybe it was from the monuments of the cemetery I'd avoided that morning. The monuments to people from a very off-kilter war.

She didn't balk at the subject. She never avoided the tough ones. "We wish we could. But whether we can see them or not, they're still there. I just consider that we might want to look at them from time to time so they can remind us never to try that path again."

"Isn't that a bit embarrassing?"

"Sure, it is. So are some tattoos. But having them there reminds us not to try that again."

I laughed. I had never heard this sort of talk from her before.

"But you never had a tattoo."

She didn't question my knowledge, just continued. "Doesn't mean I didn't consider it. But in my neck of the woods, nice girls didn't get those." We both laughed, probably remembering when I colored my own tattoo on my hand with a permanent marker.

She continued, "While I still wouldn't consider one for myself, I know that I have to stop trying to make the rest of the world agree with my thinking. Or in this case, the thinking of my childhood neighborhood. If people want a tattoo, they should get a tattoo. For the rest of us, it will just remind us that we don't want that."

"You're pretty wise."

"Wisdom is just the evidence of scars unseen."

"Who said that?"

"I did. Didn't you just hear me?"

"You just made that up?"

"Sure. I'm always coming up with my own wise sayings. But when you say it to a toddler who is wearing a mashed potato hat, it doesn't get written down. Which reminds me, I have a toddler with mashed potatoes in her hair."

"Wanda."

"How did you know her name?"

Yeah. This time she caught me. I improvised.

"You mentioned her name before."

"I don't think I did."

"Maybe Norene did."

"Okay, we'll go with that." She laughed. I really liked her laugh. It was a bit of a tinkle. Kind of like thin glass chimes in a spring breeze.

"May I call tomorrow?" I was a bit forward, but I needed some assurance.

"You may call tomorrow." I could hear the smile in her voice. I really think she was enjoying herself.

"Have a good day, Ruth."

"And you, Chris."

Chapter Seven

Mother, Daughter, Rebel

After this call, I sat in my car with Clair de Lune playing and thought back to our real-life phone calls. They had never sounded this playful. They never got this deep. And they certainly never included vibrations or tattoos.

I wish they had. We might have been friends, instead of mother and daughter. Or, better yet, added to mother and daughter. I couldn't give up that relationship.

We had been good as mother and daughter. Even if we didn't get to this depth of conversation.

I even remembered how we had always closed our phone calls. One of us would say "I love you" and the other would answer "always."

That was one of our little rituals, like the one where she always blessed my car when I left the driveway. She used to look like the pope standing there in the driveway flailing her arms in a big sign of the cross.

I loved having her as a mom. But I missed out on the chance to know her as a friend, a woman, an individual, a writer, and a bit of a rebel.

Why had it taken this long to realize that my mother was not born a mother? She was a person just like me. Who shaped me. Who created the foundation of my thoughts. The foundation I was still building on.

My scribbles in my journal were a bit frenetic after this visit. As if I were worried that, if I didn't catch them, they would be lost like thoughts from moments when a toddler wore a mashed potato hat.

It wasn't until I laid down in bed that I realized I had forgotten the shadow of the morning and the guilt over going to the phone booth instead of the cemetery.

Chapter Eight

Outdated Textbooks

The next morning the cemetery was first. It was hard because I was so ready to be on the phone. But I went and, even with the connections of the previous days, I felt a little removed.

For the first time I realized this was not a place Mom and I had shared. I remember that single time before there was a marker, we had visited the spot. We mocked the future and danced in a spot we thought was our graves. We were apparently at least five rows wrong.

But this spot. This spot had no hold over us. Neither of us had real memories attached to it. It was just the last house my parents occupied. I never shared it with them, so it wasn't our memory.

I felt like the cemetery lost a bit of its hold on me that day. And I don't think I minded. Even though the loss of this comfort zone of grief was a bit disconcerting, I think it was worth it.

I felt a bit lighter as I headed to the Gladiola. Wow. Had it always been this nasty looking? I don't know if I had noticed before that the left side was completely collapsed. It looked like a small bomb had exploded. Amazing how time took its victims even when we didn't notice.

I sauntered to the phone. Strange that I would saunter.

Everything in the last few years had either felt like a mad rush or a drudge. Saunter was an improvement. I liked sauntering. It felt like I was in control. And that was a new feeling.

The phone rang and she picked up after three rings.

"A little slower today?" I started right into the conversation.

"I decided to saunter."

My breath caught in my throat.

"Yes, I think sometimes we have to decide our own pace."

I was stunned at how connected we were. I felt like a toddler at the circus, trying to fathom the tightrope when my undeveloped mind still marveled at sidewalks.

"You know," she continued as though she had heard everything I was thinking, "sometimes we have to rethink our pace. We think we're in control, but we're just doing the things that are expected of us. When we realize we're just playing out someone else's script, it's time to slow down, saunter, and think about which script we want to act out."

"Where do you come up with this stuff?" I was amazed.

"The same place you do. The wisdom of the ages is hanging around in the air, just waiting for us to tune into it."

"Why does it take so long to find that wisdom?"

"You have to hurt. Pain is the price for true wisdom."

"Is that another one of yours?"

"It sure is. You can have it."

"I'll take it." I continued. "This isn't the topic I had in mind for today."

"Isn't it? Didn't you start our conversation?"

"Yes, but..."

"Oh, no *buts* are allowed here." She laughed, and the tinkle soothed me all over again. "Buts are just a way to try to change the direction of a conversation. We're on track and we're going to stay there."

"Okay then, the track I had planned to talk to you about today was guilt. Shame. You know, when you really feel bad that you didn't feel bad enough to do the right thing?" I realized my thoughts were still on the missed cemetery visit.

"Who's to say what the right thing is?"

"Well, there's usually an accepted right thing."

"Based on our experience."

"Right."

"But our experience is built on our influences. Who were your influences?"

I paused. How did I answer this to her? My mother. My biggest influence.

"My parents," I hedged. "Also, my teachers, religious leaders, world leaders, even my peers."

"And have any of them changed their opinions since the time you discussed issues with them?"

I thought about it. Considering that most of my biggest issues were discussed in early years, about a half century ago, I was pretty sure opinions had changed.

"Yes, I guess so."

"So, isn't there the possibility that you're working from an outdated textbook? Even encyclopedias don't stay current."

"I remember. The ones we had still mentioned about the possibility of man walking on the moon."

"So did mine." There was a pause as we made the connection. "And so, we have to accept that what might have seemed right then isn't the same kind of right now. We've grown. The world has changed. And shame is an outdated emotion that doesn't allow us to celebrate that we've grown. If we feel guilty about past events, it's a bigger problem. It means we don't think we've changed since then."

"So, I shouldn't be embarrassed about all my mistakes and the things I feel were wrong?"

"Embarrassed, maybe. That will keep you from doing them again. Improved, definitely. Especially if it makes you willing to share the experience to keep others from the same mistakes. But guilt or shame means that you haven't grown past that time and you expect it to happen again."

"But I didn't give the proper attention to something that I should have." I couldn't tell her it was her grave, could I?

"You give your attention to what matters at the moment. Your attention decides what matters. You don't. And that's good. Because sometimes we're hung up on things that we should be letting go of. If our attention wanes, maybe it's telling us it's time to move on."

"I'm not sure I'm ready."

"We're never really ready. We just have to jump and have faith that we'll learn to fly."

I sat in silence, and she seemed to sense that I had enough to think about. "I'll talk to you soon. Let me go give Christee her breakfast. If she doesn't eat on time, she gets all emotional."

"Bye."

The phone went silent. I was teary-eyed and realized I hadn't eaten breakfast, so I headed home to brunch on a frozen waffle.

Chapter Nine

Regrets

The routine continued and I loved it. I came back to life.

Even while the phone calls got shorter, the effects lasted longer. It took a while before I realized I had started going every few days instead of every day. And yet she was always there, like she'd been waiting to pick up the phone. Never angry that I hadn't called. Always delighted when I did.

It was a Friday, I think, when I finally got up the nerve to ask her about her life.

"What about you, Ruth?"

"What about me, Chris?"

"We talk about my issues, my questions, all the time. What about you?"

"I don't have any questions."

"You're that together?" I marveled.

"I'm that fulfilled. Oh wait, that sounds too high and mighty. Let's put it this way, I've gotten the answers I needed. In fact, I got some of them very recently. I don't have anything tugging at my soul to be answered now."

"Okay, let me ask. What do you hope your life accomplishes?"

"Good question. Let me think." I could hear her slow deep breath and then she began, "I hope my life sets a million fireflies out into the world to shine a little light on things that will make people feel better. I hope I live a life as a servant, not a saint. I don't want people to know my name. I just want them to live better because I put something special into action. And I want to know my children are happy and know that they are loved."

How could I answer that? I just sat there, tears dripping from my chin onto the black handset and then continuing their journey onto my shirt, my heart, and beyond.

"Chris, are you there?"

"Oh yes, ma'am."

"Ma'am? Good lord, you're calling me ma'am?"

"Sorry. Force of habit. I mean, it's just my all-purpose word."

She snorted. I had forgotten she did that when she laughed hard. "Oops. That just sneaked out. I was just thinking that using ma'am is a much better all-purpose word than some of the words people use so often."

"Oh, you mean like the bathroom wall."

"Precisely. It reminds me of a priest I knew who said *ham and eggs* instead of curse words."

I stayed on course. "So, I have to ask, if you could change something, anything, what would it be?"

"Change? Why would I change something?"

"Well, like I know you wanted to be a big-time writer. Famous, with maybe a Pulitzer or two. Or a Nobel Prize. Or lots of money. You know, the writing prizes."

"Oh my, you went straight to the heart with that one, didn't you?"

"That's what I was headed for."

She paused and I heard her breath pass across the phone. I could picture that crooked tooth on one side. The same one I have. I could imagine her scribbling with that tiny little green pen she kept by the phone. In that pause, I lived a childhood again. Then she spoke and brought me back.

"No. I'm not the famous writer I dreamed of being. I'm definitely not rich. But what I realized is that it was never about the writing itself." She slowed down, like she wanted to be sure I heard her words. "It's about living a life full of experiences worth writing about. Even if those stories, those lessons, never make it onto paper. I just didn't know the words to explain that goal in those early days. Funny for a writer to admit. I had to learn the right words for why I wanted to write."

"Do you have regrets?"

"Not anymore. I have memories instead. And they override any regrets or what I might have seen as missed opportunities.

"Did I just hear a baby?" I couldn't help connecting with the sound of the infant in the background.

"Good ear. Sounds like someone wants to complain about a tooth coming in. I need to get ready to listen for a while."

"She's a whiner, huh?" Funny to think I was talking about myself.

"No. She just experiences everything to the fullest. It will be her pain and her triumph in life."

I nodded. I thought she could hear it.

"Later, Chris."

As I walked away, I realized that the center of the old motel was looking even worse. In fact, the middle of the roof had collapsed, and it looked like the old building was about to give up the ghost.

I hated the thought of that. I wondered how I'd feel about making phone calls out in an open field once the Gladiola wasn't there to shield my phone booth from the world.

<u>Chapter Ten</u>

When I Grow Up

"So, what's our topic for today?" She started the conversation. I love that I could hear the smile in her voice.

"I don't know." I hated to admit it, but my mind was blank.

"Give me a statement about your life."

That didn't take long. It was the thing that was always at the forefront of my mind. "I don't know what I want to be when I grow up."

She laughed out loud. "You've been sitting on that one for a while, haven't you? You bounced that question out as though it were a daily thought."

"It is."

"First things first. How old did you say you were?"

I made some unintelligible mumble. She knew, anyway.

"Then I can safely say that the chance of you growing up has pretty well passed."

I snorted. Yes, I snort when I laugh, too.

"And the second problem with that statement is the word *be*." She paused and I could hear the silence, then the birds, then the wind, and then her voice again. Funny that silence is never really silent.

"We put a lot of emphasis on what we will be, don't we? But we forget that it's not about *be*. *Be* is ego. *Do* is purpose."

"Okay, you've gone a little far on me, Ruth. I'm not sure I'm getting this."

"What you want to *be* is a label. I want to be a doctor. I want to be a librarian. I want to be president. Every one of those is a label. They tell your job. They tell your supposed station in life. But they don't tell anything about you. Are you going to save people's lives? Are you going to share knowledge with the world? Are you going to encourage people to talk about peace? Those are *dos.* And honestly, you can do those no matter what your title."

"But I'm supposed to be something."

"Why?"

"Because we're supposed to have a purpose in life."

"And do you have a purpose now?"

"I think so."

"What is it?"

"I want to make a difference. That sounds so corny when I say it out loud, but it's true. I want to think I'm making people's lives better. That I'm making the world better. Oh yeah, and that I'm helping animals."

"Nice purpose." She sat silently. In fact, the silence stretched so long that I thought the connection might have been lost. Then she continued. "Having a label doesn't make your actions any more real. The label is just showing off to other people. Your purpose is those actions, and you do them because they're part of you, not because they're part of a job."

"But I'm supposed to have a career. A salary. And maybe a white picket fence around a house."

"Who decided that?"

I started to say my mother, but I knew better. However, she knew too.

"Remember, some of the things you learned are outdated views. You don't have to be rich, elected, or tenured to be a success. You have to do what you're meant to do."

"How do I know what that is?"

"How do you feel when you do something that you feel is attached to your purpose of helping people, saving animals, making the world better?"

"I feel really good." Well, that sounded lame. "I mean…"

"I know what you mean. That magical feeling. A sense of delight. That's when purpose and action match up. And that is what you're supposed to do. That is you. The rest of it is just window dressing."

"This is pretty heavy stuff," I mumbled.

She heard. "Yes, and it can also take a weight off of you. Why don't you go out there and do *you* today?"

The phone line went silent. And I went out to work on my purpose. Which probably meant I was going to end up with another stray.

My purpose sure gave me a dirty house.

Chapter Eleven

Growing Older

I hated bringing up something like aging, but I felt a need to. I hadn't been able to talk to her about it during her last days. Freeken' Alzheimer's gave me such short visits with her. And I wanted to know something. Anything. Well, I just wanted.

"Ruth, how do you feel about aging?"

"Well, there's a tiny question. Got a few years?"

"I mean, does it scare you? Does it make you want to try to freeze time?"

I listened to the baby coo in the background and could picture her looking down at little Christee.

"Oh yes. There are moments I'd like to save in a glass jar that I take down to look at on days when I know life is going to be tough.

But I also know that every moment has the potential to be one of those special ones. And if I'm spending too much time looking back over those old moments, I might just miss a new one."

"But aren't you scared about getting older? About dying?"

"Honestly," she hesitated for a moment, then continued. "Honestly, I believe that the older you get, the less hold age and death have over you."

She explained, "I look at it like this. When we were young, we constantly ran everywhere. We felt we had to get to places quickly. We hadn't realized yet that the journey was life and the places we thought were the most important goals were actually just steps along the way. As we get older, we slow down. We don't need to hurry because we want to look around us, soak the moment in, and file it away."

I laughed. "Did you know that I follow elderly drivers to protect them from the traffic behind them?"

"I'd expect nothing less from you. But don't forget to take care of you. Those elderly people didn't get that age without learning some things. They'll be okay."

"Do you think it hurts to die?" I couldn't believe I had the nerve to ask that question.

"No, dear. I don't think it hurts to die. Living holds all the parts that hurt."

Chapter Twelve

Those Who Know Us Best

On the next call I had a recent anger to share with her.

"Ruth." I started without delay. I was still riled up from an earlier phone call. "I am so angry at my family."

"Well of course you are. They're your family."

"But aren't I supposed to love them unconditionally?"

"Definitely. That doesn't mean you'll always like them. After all, they are like different versions of you."

"No way."

"Way," she parroted the word back at me. "They are so much like you that you notice their faults. That's because they're the same faults that you recognize in yourself."

"But they make me so crazy."

"Such a thin line between love and crazy."

"I thought that was between love and hate."

"I took poetic license. You will always have challenges with family, Chris. Think about it. They were there for your early mistakes and when your scars were born. They even created some of those scars. Of course, you're not going to be completely comfortable around them. Just like when you go to a class reunion and revert to the 16-year-old version of you."

"But how do I handle that?"

"There's no set rule. Some people shove down any disagreements long enough to get together with family for one meal each year. Some fight out in the open, but they're still there when needed. Some check out and watch from the outskirts. And some families actually get along. It doesn't matter. They're still family. They are part of what made you and it doesn't matter if that scares you off or pulls you near. It's just a fact."

"Should I feel guilty…"

"Whoa. I thought we already had the guilt talk. There's no such thing as guilt. There's just deciding what is right for you and doing it. And if that changes, be willing to change. Very few opinions or feelings are forever, you know."

"But how do I tell them when they drive me crazy?"

"They know. Because you'll be driving them crazy at the same exact time."

"You're pretty smart."

"I resent the *pretty* part of that statement."

"Point taken, Ruth."

"Safe travels, Chris."

Chapter Thirteen

Clearing for the Future

As I walked away, I noticed orange flags around the perimeter of the lot. I wasn't sure, but I didn't feel good about it. I asked my husband when I got home.

"Sounds like they're about to raze the building."

"Raze it?"

"Tear it town. They're going to prepare the ground for a new structure. Where did you see the flags?"

"Around the old Gladiola Motel."

"Probably a good thing. That structure is a danger these days. I'd hate to think of any kids getting into the building."

I couldn't stop thinking about it. My motel. Possibly my phone booth. Going away.

I hurried back that afternoon and sure enough, there was a crew out there.

"What's happening?" I tried to act nonchalant, but inside I was screaming.

The rumpled foreman jumped at the voice from behind him. "Oh, sorry. Didn't know there were neighbors out here."

I didn't correct him.

"We're going to clear out all the structures tomorrow afternoon. A new country club is coming to town."

"Here?"

"Yep. Going to be a really nice development. If you own land out here, I guarantee your property value is going to rise." He smiled a toothy grin as if that fixed everything.

I just fake smiled like that was the best news in the world and drove off.

Chapter Fourteen

Connection Issues

The next morning, I was out earlier than ever before. Still dark. A bit spooky. Didn't matter. I needed to talk to Ruth. I needed to talk to Mom.

"You're calling early," she answered on the first half ring.

"They're…" I choked. "They're disconnecting my phone today."

"Don't let that bother you." She paused. "You don't really need to spend time on the phone. You need to be writing."

"But I won't be able to talk to you."

You don't need me, Chris. You got this."

"But you're my best friend."

"Sounds like it's time to make some new ones."

"I don't…" I started. But I stopped.

"I know. It's hard to let go of your security blanket. Linus knew."

"Yeah." I just didn't know what to say.

In the moment of silence, I heard the sound of the infant Christee.

"Oh dear. Baby's crying. Time for a diaper change. That girl goes all the time."

"I have the same problem."

"Ha." Her laugh was cut off by the renewed cry of the baby.

Chapter Fifteen

The Final Advice

There was a pause on the line. Then she sighed deeply.

"My last advice to you is this. You have pain. Deep pain that takes your breath away sometimes. You need to write it. Leave it on the page. Other people might even learn from it.

But it doesn't really matter whether anyone else gets it. It's for you.

Be true to your heart. Never lie to the page."

She paused, apparently weighing her words, and then continued a little more slowly.

"You will get pulled off course. Distracted by both monumental and microscopic moments. That's to be expected. That's also where you'll find the most important discoveries."

"You think so?"

"I know so. Sometimes those discoveries are heartbreaking. Other times they're just what that broken heart needs. One of the times I got pulled off course was this amazing little soul with a full diaper. And I wouldn't change that for anything. She made my life come full circle."

She laughed softly and then said the words I had always dreamed of hearing. "I had six children. I love them all. But I think I was waiting for her all the time."

"I know she's a lucky little girl." I couldn't hold back the tears.

"I know she won't feel like that at times."

"She'll know. Even when you have to chew her out. She'll know. And I hope you don't hold it against her if she does something like break your favorite glass Christmas ornament. I'm sure she thought she was just trying to make it shine. You know how kids overdo things when they're trying to say *I love you* without words."

Silence.

"Mom."

"Yes, dear."

"I love you."

A pause. Then she responded as I prayed she would.

"Always."

And the line clicked dead.

But I was alive again. I returned to the blank page and typed the title.

Calling Home.

#

Note from the author:

Thank you for sharing this journey with me. I hope that you have found messages that speak to you in these pages.

Because I usually lean toward comedy in my writing, this is the most unusual thing that I have ever written, and it has actually changed the course of my life. I hope it makes a positive difference in your life as well.

If you feel this book will be a positive influence for others, please consider leaving a review on Amazon to help readers find it.

And if you'd like to continue our connection, you can find me on most social media platforms or at

www.Christee.net or
Christee.Atwood@gmail.com.

Thank you for the precious gift of your time.

#ForOurMothers

Made in the USA
Columbia, SC
05 June 2022

61311007R00048